3

© Snap Productions Ltd

8 Reservoir Road, Birkenhead, CH42 8LJ

Printed 2010

Designed by Bag of Badgers

ISBN 978-0-9566075-2-2

1 3 5 7 9 10 8 6 4 2

Printed in China

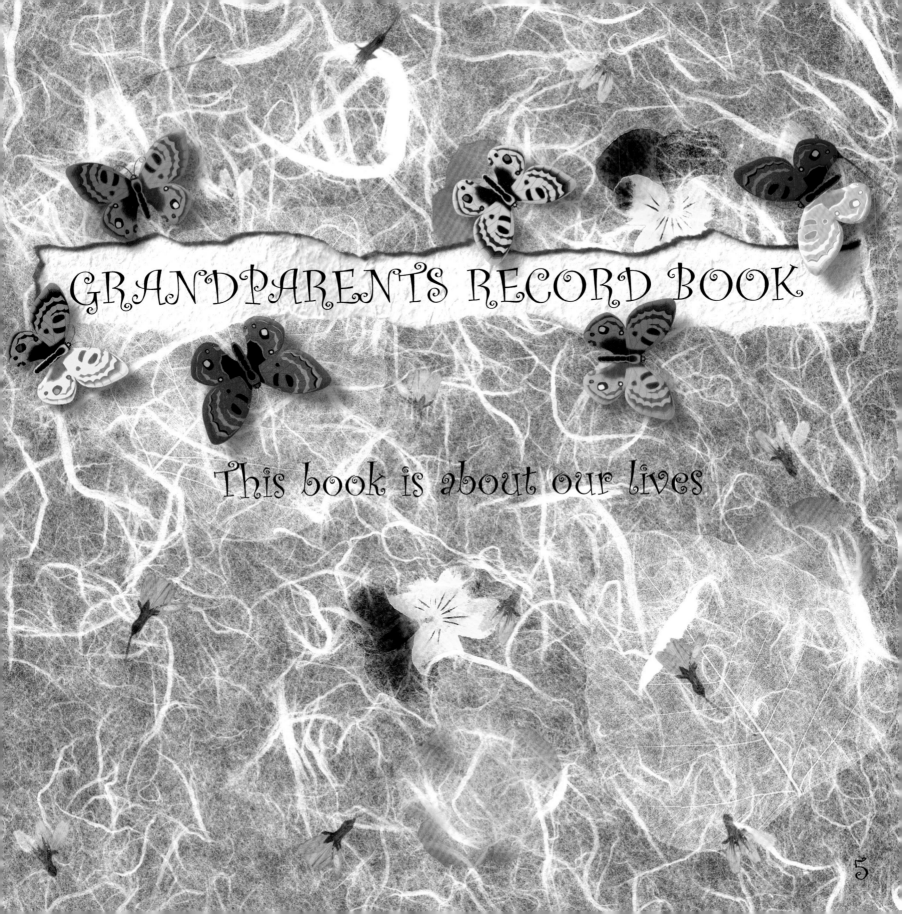

GRANDPARENTS RECORD BOOK

This book is about our lives

Grandmother's name:

What I am called by my grandchildren:

My date of birth:

6

Grandfather's name:

What I am called by my grandchildren:

My date of birth:

Our family tree

Father - D.O.B / D.O.D   Mother - D.O.B / D.O.D   Father - D.O.B / D.O.D   Mother - D.O.B / D.O.D

Father - D.O.B / D.O.D   Mother - D.O.B / D.O.D

Siblings and Children: ——————————— Grandmother's name - D.O.B

Children and Partners - D.O.B

Grandchildren - D.O.B.

Father - D.O.B / D.O.D   Mother - D.O.B / D.O.D   Father - D.O.B / D.O.D   Mother - D.O.B / D.O.D

Father - D.O.B / D.O.D   Mother - D.O.B / D.O.D

Grandfather's name - D.O.B ———————— Siblings and Children:

Our parents and grandparents

GRANDMOTHER
What I called my Mother and Father:

The jobs they had:

How my Mother and Father met:

Their ages when they got married:

What my Mother enjoyed doing:

What my Father enjoyed doing:

My favourite memories of my Mother:

My favourite memories of my Father:

Where my Grandparents lived when
I was growing up:

My Mother's parents' jobs were:

My Father's parents' jobs were:

What I remember about
my Grandparents

My parents

GRANDFATHER
What I called my Mother and Father:

The jobs they had:

How my Mother and Father met:

Their ages when they got married:

What my Mother enjoyed doing:

What my Father enjoyed doing:

My favourite memories of my Mother:

My favourite memories of my Father:

Where my Grandparents lived when I was growing up:

My Mother's parents' jobs were:

My Father's parents' jobs were:

What I remember about my Grandparents:

My parents

When we were born

GRANDMOTHER
Where I was born:

How old my Mother was when
I was born:

How old my Father was when
I was born:

Why my parents chose my name:

Anything I was told about my birth:

What I was like as a baby:

Me as a baby

GRANDFATHER
Where I was born:

How old my Mother was when
I was born:

How old my Father was when
I was born:

Why my parents chose my name:

Anything I was told about my birth:

What I was like as a baby:

Our siblings

GRANDMOTHER
My brothers and sisters:

How many years between us:

Who I shared a bedroom with:

Games we enjoyed playing:

How we got on together:

Favourite childhood memories
of my siblings:

What they did when they left home:

What jobs they had as adults:

How we got on together as adults:

Memories of my siblings as adults:

A picture of me with

GRANDFATHER
My brothers and sisters:

How many years between us:

Who I shared a bedroom with:

Games we enjoyed playing:

How we got on together:

Favourite childhood memories
of my siblings:

What they did when they left home:

What jobs they had as adults:

How we got on together as adults:

Memories of my siblings as adults:

A picture of me with

Growing up

GRANDMOTHER

Where I grew up:

My earliest memory:

Memories of my childhood home:

Me aged

Best memories of my childhood:

My favourite toys:

Worst memories of my childhood:

My favourite games:

What I was like as a teenager:

How I got on with my parents:

What sort of food I ate:

GRANDFATHER

Where I grew up:

My earliest memory:

Memories of my childhood home:

My favourite toys:

My favourite games:

How I got on with my parents:

What sort of food I ate:

Me aged

Best memories of my childhood:

Worst memories of my childhood:

What I was like as a teenager:

17

School days

GRANDMOTHER

Name and location of:

My first school:

My secondary school:

My best friends at school:

My favourite teacher and why:

My worst teacher and why:

My favourite subject:

My worst subject:

The biggest trouble I got into at school:

How I was punished:

School teams I was part of:

School plays I took part in:

Biggest achievements at school:

How many exams I gained:

How old I was when I left school:

Good and bad memories of my time at school:

GRANDFATHER

Name and location of:

My first school:

My secondary school:

My best friends at school:

My favourite teacher and why:

My worst teacher and why:

My favourite subject:

My worst subject:

The biggest trouble I got into at school:

How I was punished:

School teams I was part of:

School plays I took part in:

Biggest achievements at school:

How many exams I gained:

How old I was when I left school:

Good and bad memories of my time at school:

Our early days together

How old we both were when we met:

Grandmother:

Grandfather:

Where we were when we met:

How we got together:

Things we had in common:

Some activities we enjoyed doing together:

Things we didn't like about each other
Grandmother:

Grandfather:

What we liked best about each other:
Grandmother:

Grandfather:

How long we were together
before we got engaged:

How old we were when we
got engaged:
Grandmother:
Grandfather:

What our parents thought of us
getting married:
Grandmother:

Grandfather:

Best memories of the time we shared
before we were married:

A picture of us together in

21

Our wedding

The date:

The time:

The location of the ceremony:

The location of the reception:

What the groom wore on the day:

What the groom wore in the evening:

What the bride wore on the day:

What the bride wore in the evening:

Bridesmaids:

Page boys:

Ushers:

Best man:

How many guests came:

The food we ate:

Some memories of the day:

First dance/special song:

Where we stayed on our wedding night:

Where we went on our honeymoon:

Becoming parents

Our feelings on becoming parents:

Where we lived when we
decided to have children:

Our jobs before we had children:
Grandmother:

Grandfather:

How long after our marriage our
first child was born:

Our ages when our first child was born:
Grandmother:
Grandfather:

Where our children were born:

The proud parents with

How our lives changed when we
became parents:

Favourite memories of our children's
early years:

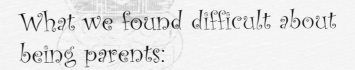

What we found difficult about
being parents:

Holidays

The type of holidays I had as a child:
Grandmother:

Grandfather:

People we went on holiday with
as a child:
Grandmother:

Grandfather:

Memories of our holidays as a child:
Grandmother:

Grandfather:

Trips I took before I was married:
Grandmother:

Grandfather:

The first holiday we went on together was to:

Memories of the holiday:

Our first holiday as parents:

Memories of the holiday:

Our favourite holiday ever and why:
Grandmother:

Grandfather:

Our worst holiday ever and why:
Grandmother:

Grandfather:

Places we'd like to go to but haven't yet:

On holiday in

Working life

GRANDMOTHER

What job I wanted to do when I was growing up:

Part-time jobs I did when I was growing up for pocket money:

Any extra training for work after leaving school:

My first full-time job:

Location of my first job:

My first wages were:

How old I was when I got my first job:

What I liked about it:

Other jobs I have had:

My favourite job and why:

My worst job and why:

If I could have another chance the career I would have chosen and why:

GRANDFATHER

What job I wanted to do when I was growing up:

Part-time jobs I did when I was growing up for pocket money:

Any extra training for work after leaving school:

My first full-time job:

Location of my first job:

My first wages were:

How old I was when I got my first job:

What I liked about it:

Other jobs I have had:

My favourite job and why:

My worst job and why:

If I could have another chance the career I would have chosen and why:

Me at work

Hobbies

GRANDMOTHER
Hobbies I enjoyed as a child:

People I shared these activities with:

Awards I achieved for
childhood activities:

Hobbies I enjoyed as a teenager:

Memorable achievements:

Other activities I enjoyed as a teenager:

People I shared these activities with:

Music I enjoyed as a teenager:

New things I began as an adult:

Who I share these activities with:

Radio and television programmes I
enjoyed as a child:

Radio and television programmes I
have enjoyed as an adult:

My favourite:
film:
book:
game:

GRANDFATHER
Hobbies I enjoyed as a child:

People I shared these activities with:

Music I enjoyed as a teenager:

People I shared these activities with:

New things I began as an adult:

Awards I achieved for
childhood activities:

Who I share these activities with:

Hobbies I enjoyed as a teenager:

Radio and television programmes I
enjoyed as a child:

Memorable achievements:

Radio and television programmes I
have enjoyed as an adult:

Other activities I enjoyed as a teenager:

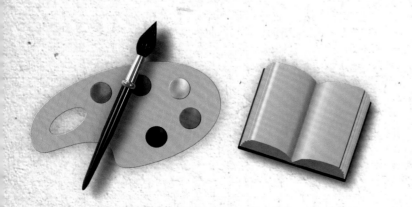

My favourite:
film:
book:
game:

Friends

My best friend as a child, and how we met:
Grandmother:

Grandfather:

Activities we enjoyed together:
Grandmother:

Grandfather:

Favourite memories of my childhood friends:
Grandmother:

Grandfather:

New friends I met as a teenager and activities we shared:
Grandmother:

Grandfather:

Friends we met as a couple:

Why I have got on
so well with them:

Grandmother:

How we met:

Grandfather:

Activities we have shared:

My best friend throughout my life
has been:
Grandmother:

Grandfather:

Us with

Christmas - then and now

How Christmas was celebrated
when I was a child:
Grandmother:

Grandfather:

Who else we shared our Christmas
with as children:
Grandmother:

Grandfather:

Our first Christmas together was:

Other people with whom we shared
our first Christmas:

How we celebrated:

34

The first Christmas presents we
bought each other:

Our best ever
Christmas and why:

How we celebrated
Christmas with our own children:

Our worst ever Christmas and why:

Other people who have spent
Christmas with us in the past:

Unusual places we have
celebrated Christmas:

Christmas in

Looking back

The most memorable historical event of our lifetime:

My biggest regret:
Grandmother:

Grandfather:

The achievement of which I am most proud:
Grandmother:

Things I would do differently:
Grandmother:

Grandfather:

Grandfather:

Looking to the future

How old we were when we became
Grandparents for the first time:

Grandmother:
Grandfather:

How we felt becoming Grandparents
for the first time:

What advice we would give to
our Grandchildren:

Fears we have for our
Grandchildren's future:

What we think our Grandchildren
will be when they grow up:

Our greatest wishes for our
Grandchildren's future: